WHEN I'm AFRAID

written and illustrated
by
JANE AARON

Golden Books
NEW YORK

Golden Books®

888 Seventh Avenue
New York, NY 10106

Designed by Gwen Petruska Gürkan

Manufactured in the United States of America

10 9 8 7 6 5 4 3 2 1

Library of Congress Cataloging-in-Publication Data
Aaron, Jane.
      When I'm afraid / written and illustrated by Jane Aaron.
           p.   cm. — (The language of parenting : 1)
      "A parent's guide to fear by Barbara Gardiner" : p.
      Summary: Explains fear as a normal part of life and discusses how
      to deal with it. Includes a parent's guide in a question-and-answer
      format with examples and suggestions.
      ISBN 0-307-44057-5 (hardcover : alk. paper)
      1. Fear in children—Juvenile literature.   2. Parenting.
      [1. Fear.]   I. Gardiner, Barbara. Parent's guide to fear.
      II. Title.   III. Series.
      BF723.F4A27   1998
      152.4'6—dc21   98-12720
                                    CIP   AC

To Timothy and Skip.

Sometimes I feel afraid

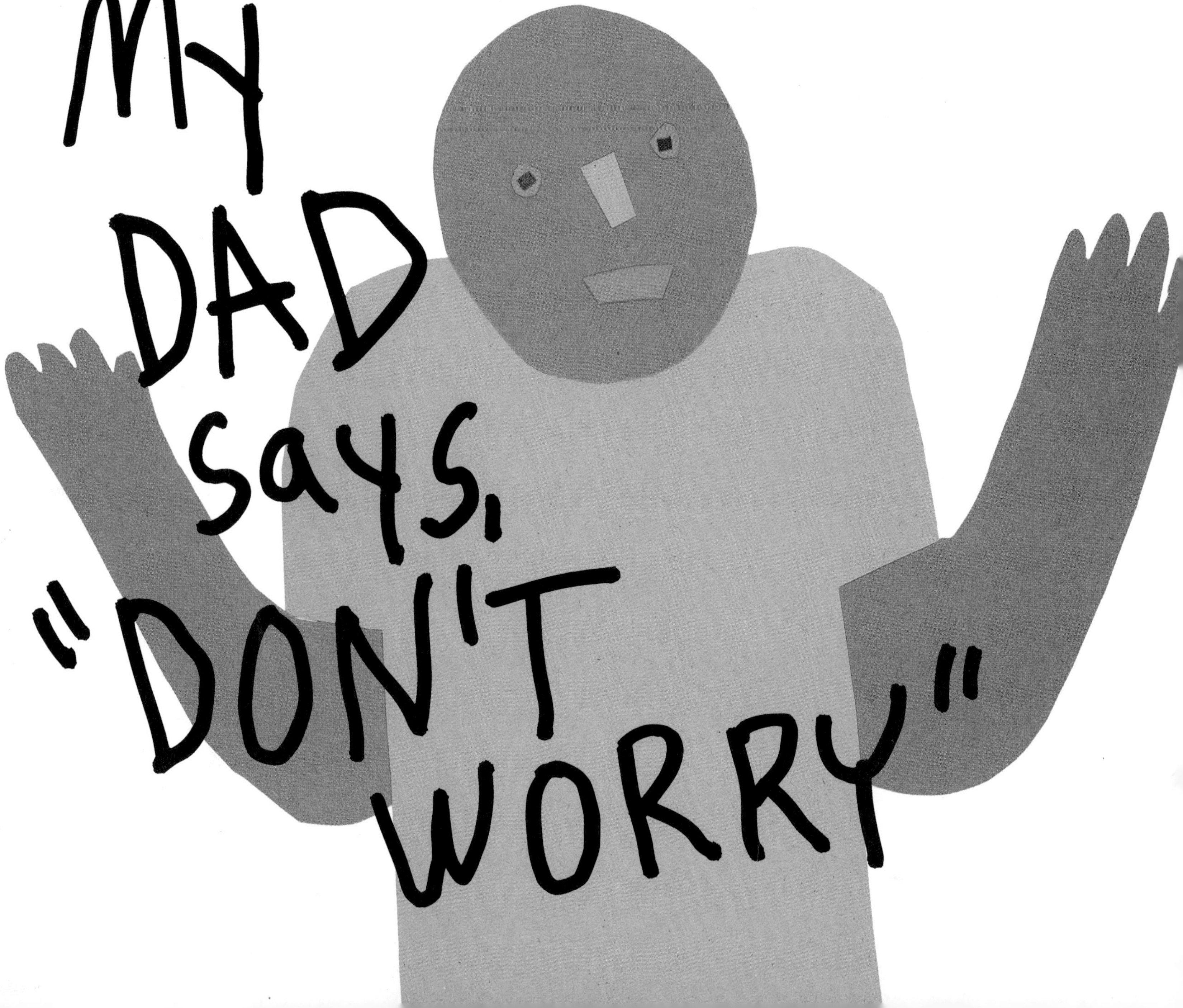

My DAD says, "DON'T WORRY"

My mom says, "There's nothing to be AFRAID of"

BUT I STILL FEEL

SCARED

Sometimes I'm afraid of new places

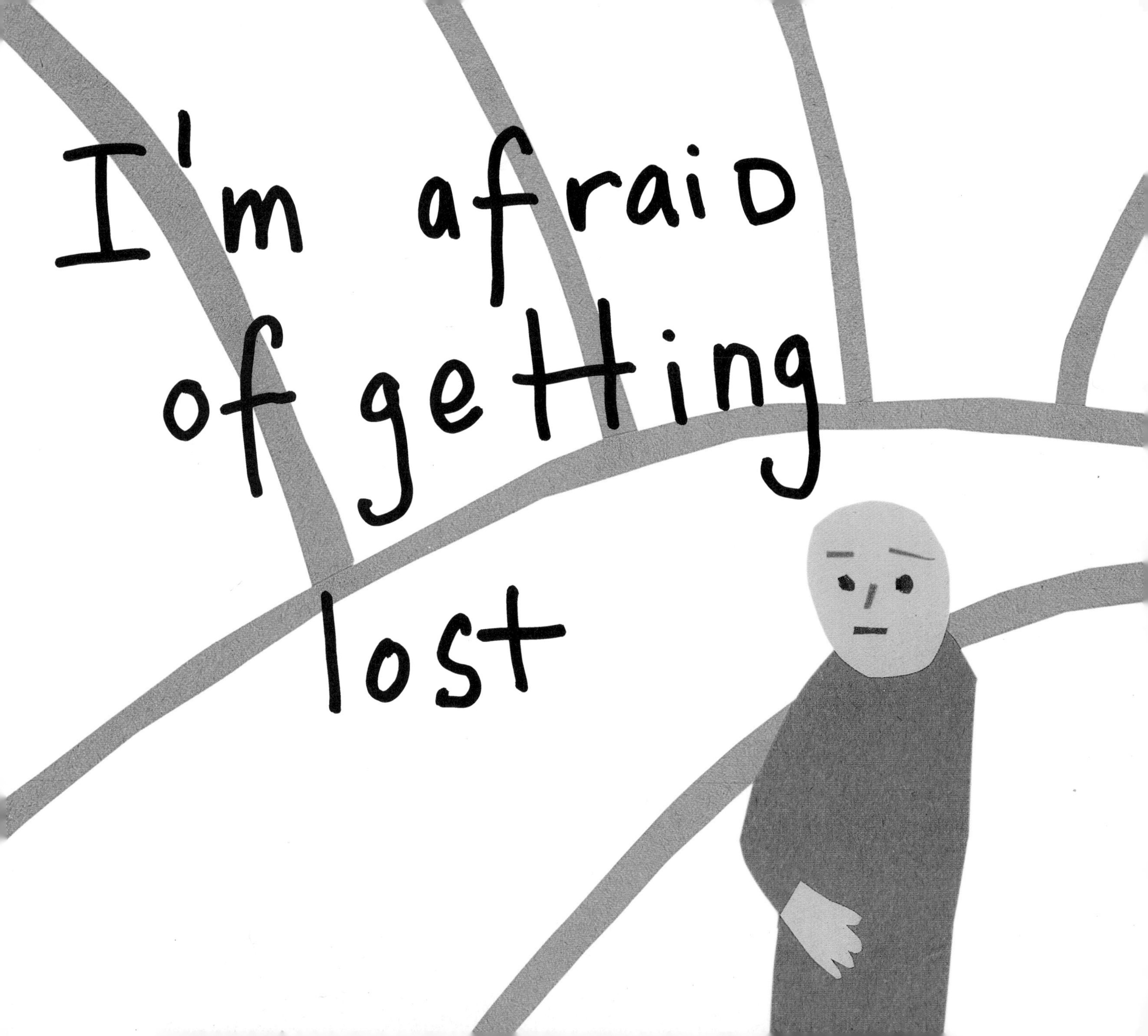
I'm afraid
of getting
lost

What if my MOM can't find me?

My
"Don't

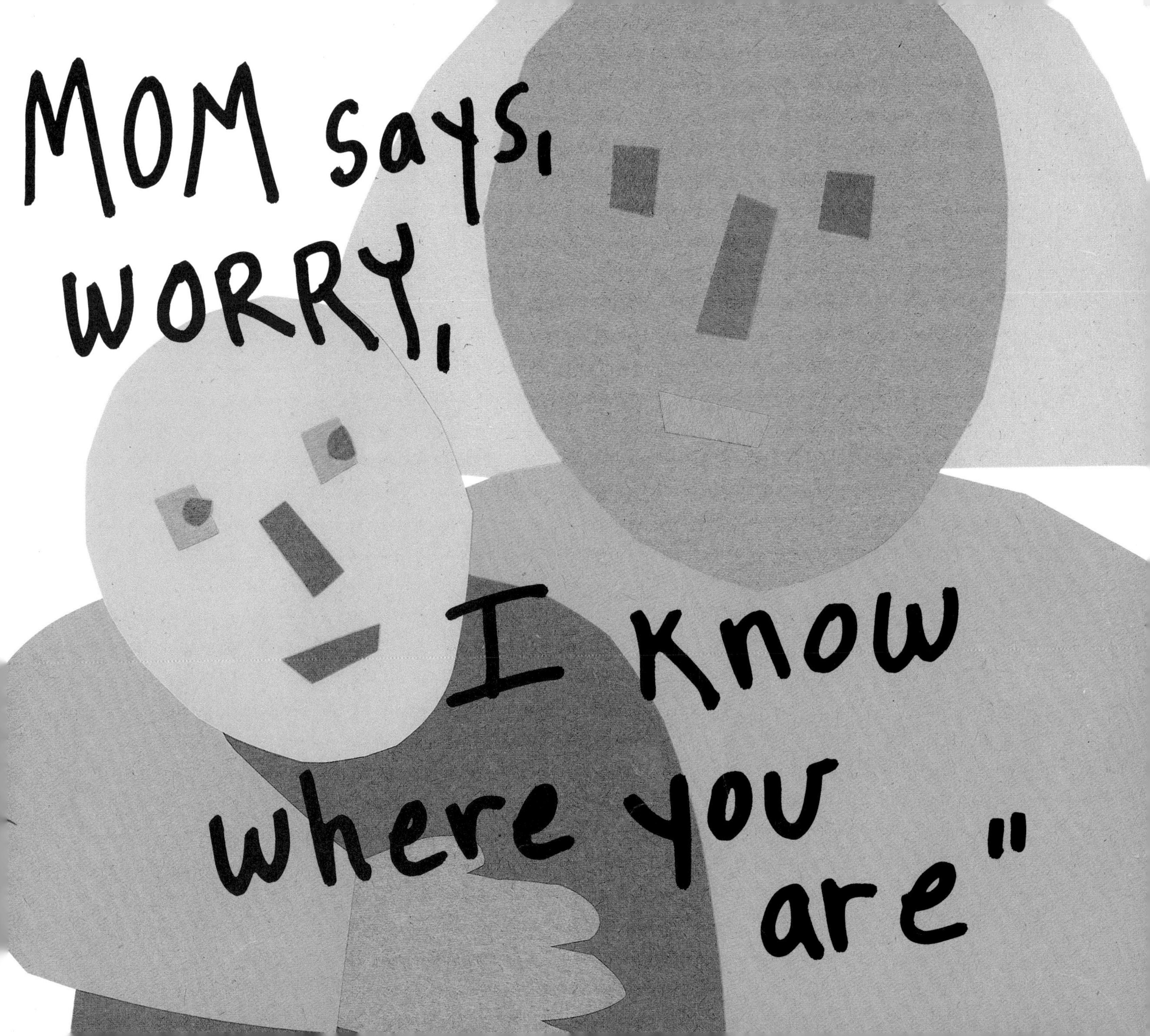
MOM says,
WORRY,
I know
where you
are"

I feel SAFE holding her hand

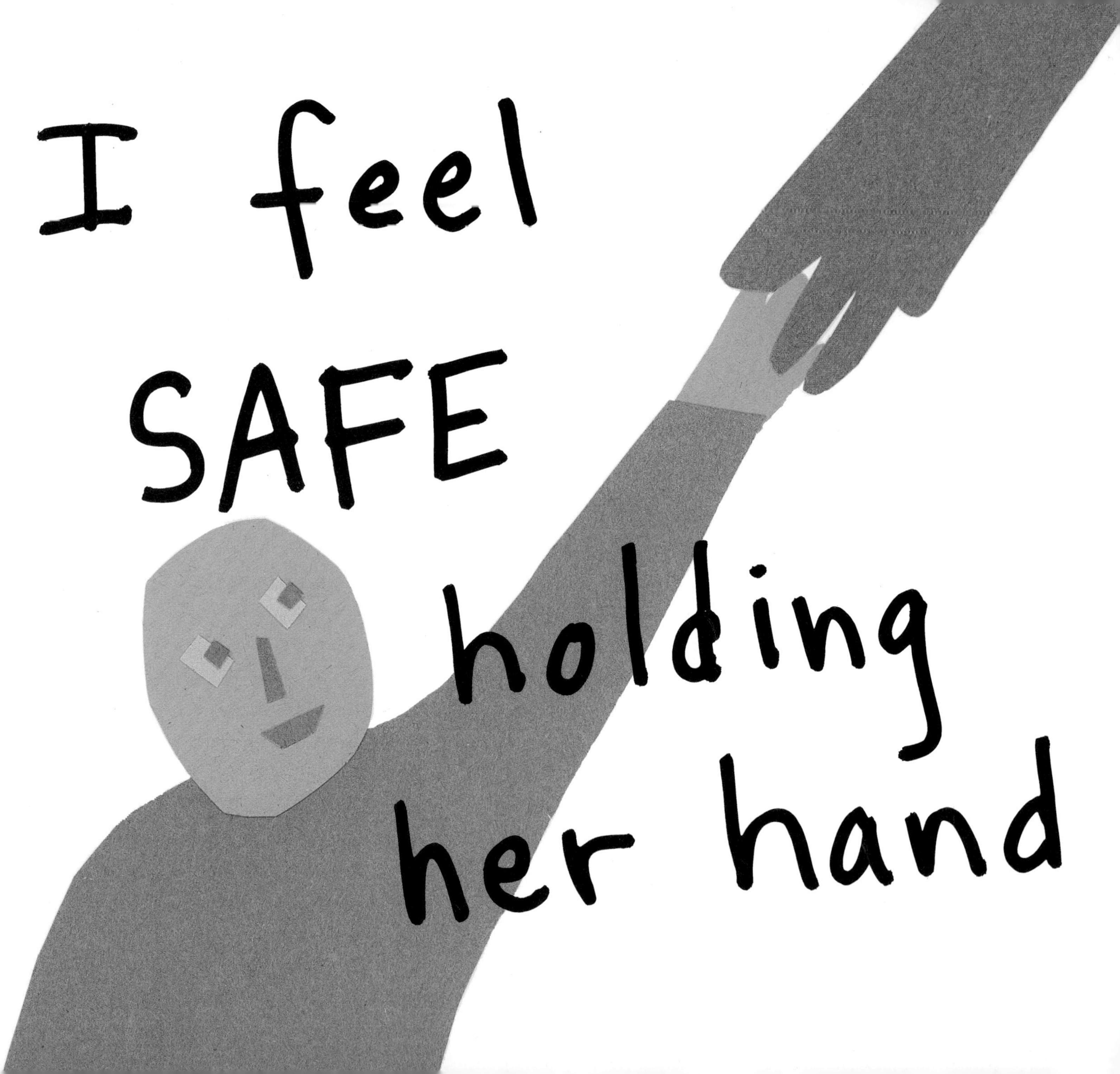

I feel scared when I have to go to the DOCTOR

I'm
afraiD
of getting
a SHOT

MY DAD SAYS

it might hurt

I'm glad when the visit is over

and I get
to choose
a STICKER

Sometimes I feel scared in my bed at night

I hear strange noises

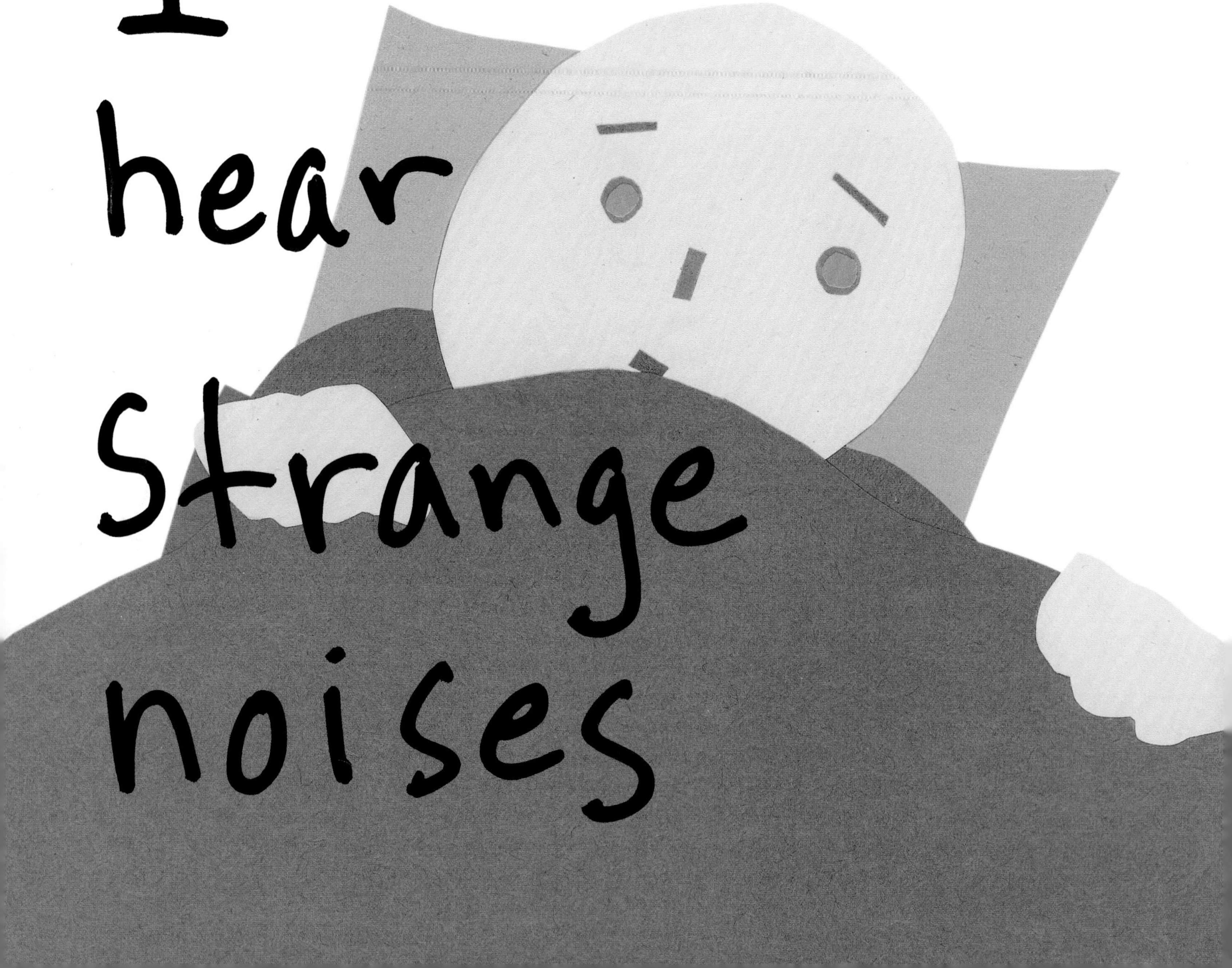

and I
think
about
MONSTERS

I call my Mom

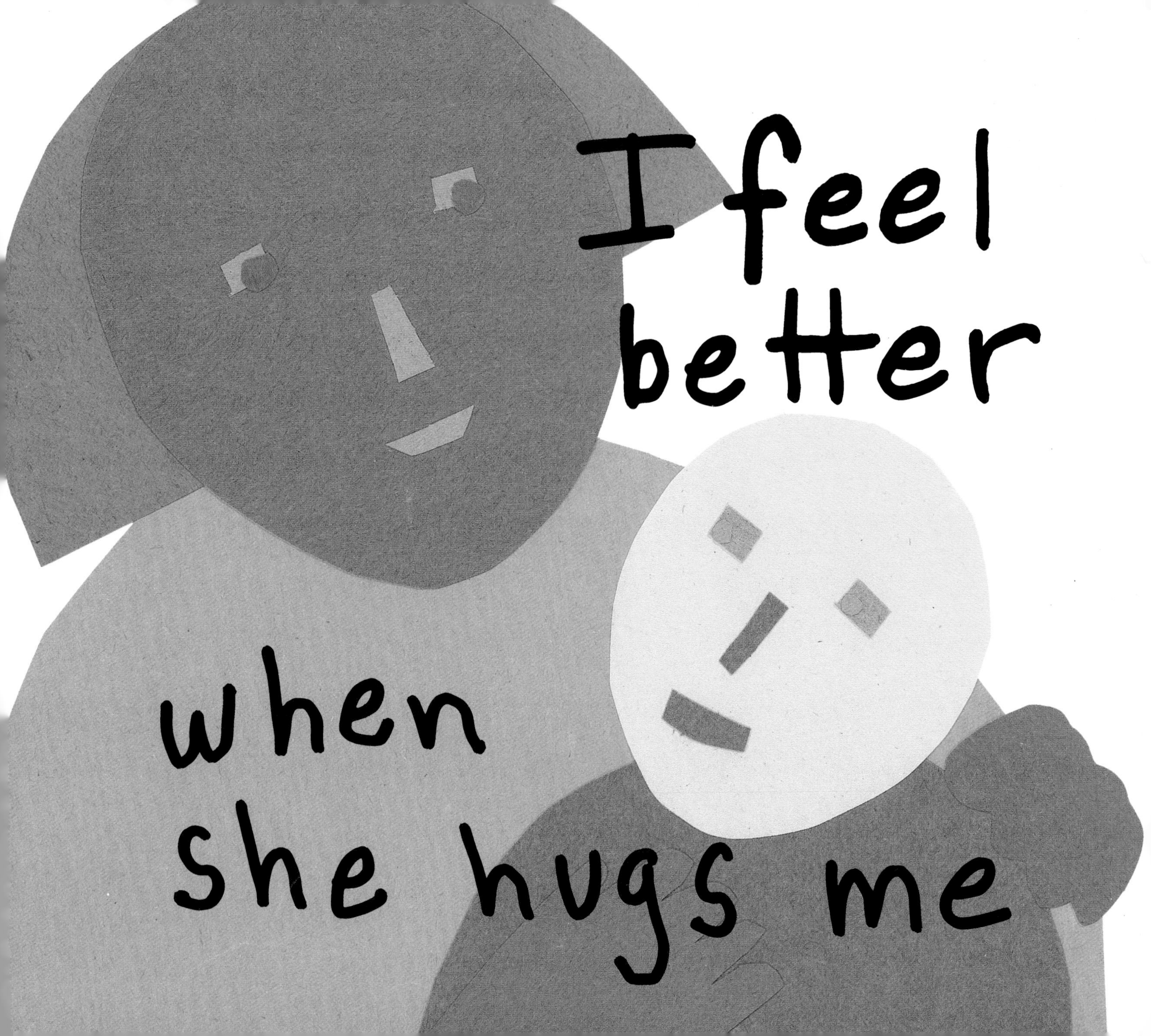

I feel better when she hugs me

gets
scareD
sometimes"

My dad says,

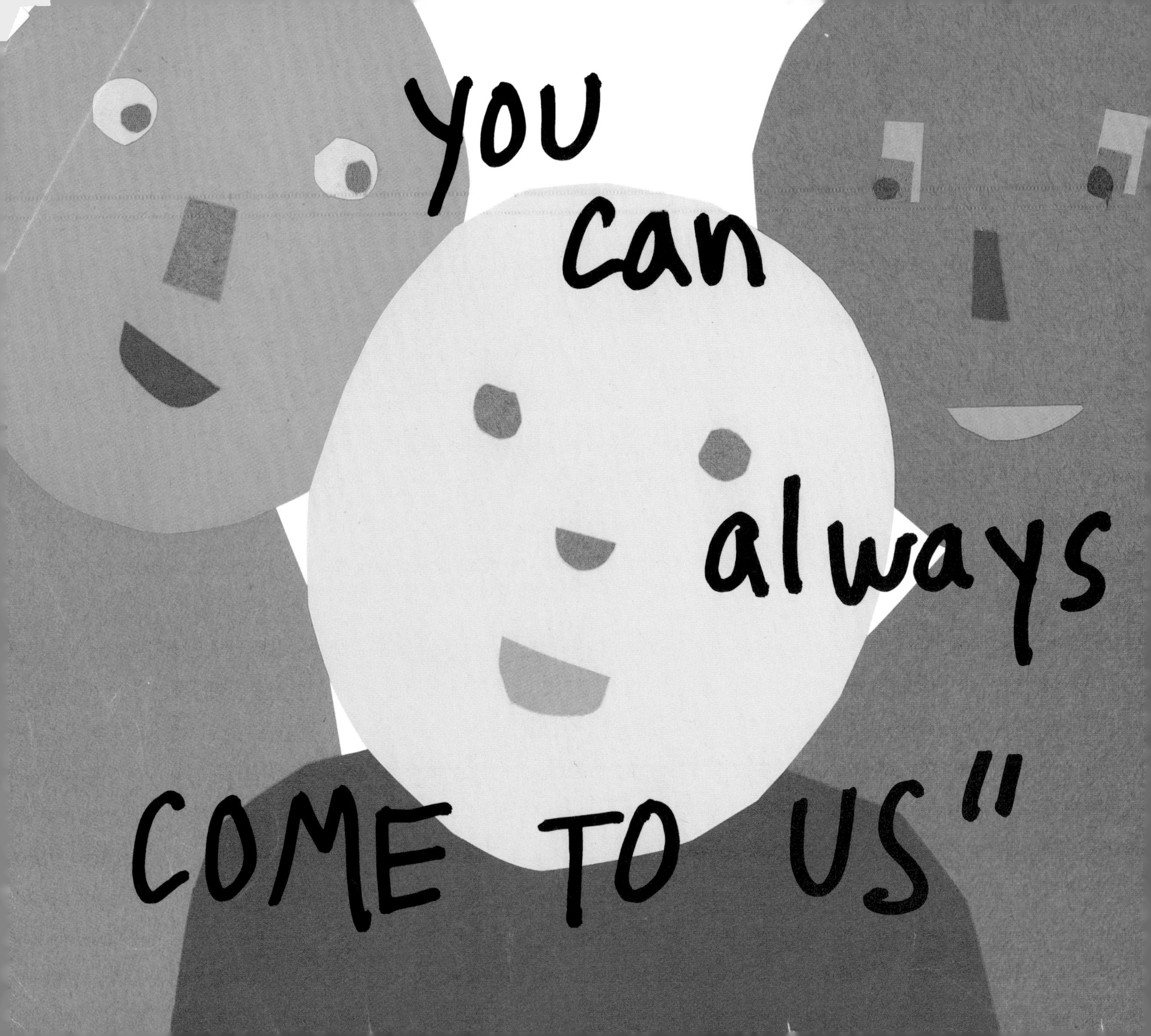
you
can
always
COME TO US"